Plays for Assembly and PSE

CHOICES

Gordon Aspland

SOUTHGATE

First published 1999 by Southgate Publishers Ltd

Southgate Publishers Ltd
15 Barnfield Avenue
Exmouth
Devon EX8 2QE

Printed and bound in Great Britain by Bell & Bain Ltd, Glasgow.

British Library Cataloguing in Publication Data.
A CIP catalogue record for this book is available from the British Library.

ISBN 1–85741–044–0

CONTENTS

INTRODUCTION

This book of short plays comes after the success of the four books of short stories published so far: *Feelings*, *Choices*, *Situations* and *Starting Out*. The stories have had a number of uses including whole school and class assemblies, story writing in Language work and Personal and Social Education (PSE). The development of the Literacy Hour has meant that there is a need for suitable material for group reading by the children themselves. '*Plays for PSE*' has been written with this in mind, both providing group reading texts for the Literacy Hour and fulfilling the needs of PSE for children to be more pro-active in looking at their behaviour towards other people.

The plays can stand alone or be used after reading the appropriate story from the original book. The latter use helps the children to get very quickly into the pace and style of the play. The plays should take no more than ten minutes to read. I found that children need to read them twice, the first time to get a feel for the language and the second time to read with expression. I have given some readers two characters. This is because I have kept to a format of groups of five readers but in somc stories I have needed more than five characters in order to keep the plot flowing. Some of these characters only have a few lines, so it is important for a reader to have two characters who appear at different times in a play, in order to feel a part of the play all the way through.

I have introduced an element of reading ability in the plays so that children of differing abilities can join together, something that does not happen too often in the Literacy Hour but is important in PSE. It is a very crude ability range based on sentence structure and vocabulary:

✤ reading age of about 6/7years
✤✤ reading age of about 8/9 years
✤✤✤ reading age of about 10/11+

The plays could be used purely as a Literacy Hour group reading session or within an extended PSE lesson using the discussion points and further activity. The plays could be acted out for the rest of the class or in a school assembly.

G. Aspland

TEACHER'S NOTES

Play 1: SAY 'NO' TO STRANGERS

Characters	*Reading Ability*	*Characters*	*Reading Ability*
Narrator	✤✤✤	Johnny	✤✤✤
Sereena	✤✤	Prakesh	✤✤
Mum/Stranger	✤		

GROUP DISCUSSION:
What did Sereena do wrong?
What should she have done?
How did the boys manage to scare the man off?

ACTIVITY:
a) The police usually ask for a written statement describing what happened. Choose a character and write a statement from their point of view.
b) Make up a description of the man. Here are some suggestions.
What kind of hair did he have? (colour, length, greasy, etc.)
What kind of clothes was he wearing? (style, colour)
Did he wear any jewellery?
How old was he?
What about the rest of his head? (ears, nose, beard, moustache, etc.)

Play 2: THE LOST MONEY

Characters	*Reading Ability*	*Characters*	*Reading Ability*
Narrator	✤✤✤	Prakesh/Father	✤✤
Mark	✤✤	Mr Blackmore/	
Mother	✤	Shop Assistant	✤✤

GROUP DISCUSSION:
What do you think about Mark's decision initially to keep the money?
What made him decide to give it back?
Mark told the shopkeeper that he'd found the money that morning. Why do you think he lied?
If Mark had kept the money what problems would he have had? Is this stealing?

ACTIVITY:
'Finders keepers, losers weepers' is a catch phrase. What does it mean?
'Honesty pays' is another catchphrase. What does it mean?
Write down some more catch phrases and test others to see if they know what they mean.

Play 3: THE SMASHED PLANT

Characters	*Reading Ability*	*Characters*	*Reading Ability*
Narrator/Colin	✤✤✤		

Nina	✤✤	Mrs Jones	✤✤
Sereena	✤	Pauline	✤

GROUP DISCUSSION:
When do you think Nina should have made a different choice of action?
Who gave Nina the right advice?
What do you think would be a fair punishment for Nina?
Why was Colin blamed? What does 'Give a dog a bad name' mean?
How does this apply to Colin?

ACTIVITY:
We all have accidents. Make up a play about an accident and show how important it is to say 'sorry' afterwards.

Play 4: THE DINNER LADY

Characters	*Reading Ability*	*Characters*	*Reading Ability*
Narrator	✤✤✤		
Mrs Jones/Nina	✤✤	Mark/Mr Hall	✤✤
Mrs MacFee	✤	Colin	✤

GROUP DISCUSSION:
Do you think it is fair that Mr Hall should cancel the camp?
Whose fault was it? Was it just one person or a group?
Why do we need dinner ladies in school?

ACTIVITY:
The school is a very busy community with many people working in it. Make a list of all the people who work and help in the school, both regularly and occasionally. Write down what they do for you.

Play 5: ONE TIN OF BAKED BEANS

Characters	*Reading Ability*	*Characters*	*Reading Ability*
Narrator	✤✤✤		
Pauline	✤✤	Mr Petrowski	✤✤
Sereena/Teacher	✤	Father/Colin	✤

GROUP DISCUSSION:
What is 'peer group' pressure?
In what ways did Pauline feel this pressure?
In what ways can you feel this pressure?
What were Pauline's feelings when they were walking up Mr Petrowski's path to give him his box of food?
Why did Pauline thank Mr Petrowski at the end?

ACTIVITY:
Make a list of the gifts you can give people that cost little or no money.

Play 1

SAY 'NO' TO STRANGERS

CHARACTERS

Narrator
Mum/Stranger
Prakesh
Sereena
Johnny

SETTING

Sereena is setting out to visit her friend, Pauline. The boys, Prakesh and Johnny are on the way home from the rec after playing football.

Sereena: I'm going out now, Mum!

Mum: Where are you going?

Sereena: I'm going to pop over to Pauline's. She wants to show me the new trainers she bought yesterday.

Mum: Don't be late. I want you home by five o'clock.

Sereena: Don't worry, I'll be back by then.

Mum: Take care crossing the road!

Sereena: Mum, I wish you'd stop nagging. I know how to cross a road! Goodbye.

Narrator: Sereena hurried out of the house. Her mum was always nagging her about walking along the streets on her own. But she made sure she looked both ways when she crossed the road. Just as she reached the other side a car passed her. It slowed down and stopped. Then it reversed up the road to where Sereena was.

Stranger: Excuse me. Can you tell me the way to the High Street?

Narrator: The man was leaning across the passenger seat, calling to Sereena through the open window.

Sereena: Well, yes, but it's a bit complicated from here.

Stranger: I'm really late for an appointment. Can you show me on this map how to get there?

Narrator: The stranger opened the passenger door and began to unfold a map on the seat.

Stranger: Please help me. I'm going to be very late.

Narrator: Sereena didn't know what to do. She remembered what the teacher had said at school about talking to strangers. But the man seemed okay. Anyway she wasn't going to get into the car.

Sereena: Okay. I think you need to turn round and go back the other way. There's the High Street.

Narrator: Sereena leaned into the car and pointed to a spot on the map. As she did so the stranger grabbed her arm.

Sereena: Let go of me, you're hurting my arm!

Stranger: Get into the car. Then I'll let go.

Narrator: As the man tried to pull Sereena across the seat of the car, her brother, Prakesh, and his friend Johnny came round the corner.

Prakesh: That was a good game, it's a pity we had to stop.

Johnny: Yeah, sorry, but I've got to go shopping for a new pair of shoes. My old ones are falling apart. It's the only time Mum can get time off work.

Prakesh: You scored a good goal. Mark couldn't get anywhere near it.

Johnny: Wasn't it funny when he dived the wrong way and got all muddy!

Prakesh: I don't think he minded. He likes getting muddy.

Johnny: He's always getting muddy. If I went home like that my Mum'd kill me.

Prakesh: Mine too!

Johnny: Hey, isn't that your sister over there, talking to that man in the car?

Prakesh: I think you're right. I wonder who he is?

Johnny: Look! He's pulling her into his car!

Prakesh: Come on! We've got to help her!

Johnny: Hey you, let go of her!

Prakesh: Let go of my sister! Help, help!

Narrator: The boys ran over to the car. Prakesh tried to pull his sister out while Johnny banged on the car roof. He tried to make as much noise as he could.

Sereena: Help me, Prakesh! He's trying to take me away!

Prakesh: Let go of my sister!

Stranger: Clear off, she said she'd help me.

Sereena: I didn't. Ow! He's hurting me!

Johnny: Help, help, this man is trying to take Sereena away!

Narrator: The man was pulling Sereena and trying to shut the car door at the same time. Prakesh was holding onto Sereena tightly. Johnny shouted as loudly as he could. He continued banging on the roof of the car.

Stranger: Hey, stop doing that. Leave my car alone.

Johnny: Let her go then.

Stranger: Push off the lot of you!

Narrator: The man let go of Sereena's arm. She and Prakesh fell out of the car and onto the pavement. The man slammed the passenger door shut and raced off down the road. The two children got to their feet.

Prakesh: Are you all right, Sereena?

Sereena: I think so. My arm hurts though.

Prakesh: What are you doing, Johnny?

Johnny: I'm trying to memorise his licence plate number. The police can trace him if they have it.

Prakesh: That's a good idea. Come on, let's get home and tell Mum.

Narrator: The three children ran to Sereena's home. Her mother was very worried to see them looking so upset.

Mum: What's the matter?

Prakesh: A man tried to drag Sereena into his car.

Mum: Darling, are you all right?

Sereena: He was horrible, Mum. He pretended to be lost and he wanted me to show him the way on a map. Then he grabbed me.

Johnny: Wasn't it lucky we came along just at that moment?

Prakesh: I pulled her out while Johnny bashed the roof of the car and made a lot of noise.

Johnny: Oh quick, have you got a piece of paper? I know the car's licence number.

Mum: Good boy. I'll telephone the police at once. Maybe they'll catch that horrible man.

Play 2

THE LOST MONEY

CHARACTERS

Narrator **Mark**
Father/Prakesh **Mother**
Shop Assistant/Mr Blackmore

SETTING

Prakesh has come over to play
in Mark's garden.

Mother: Hello Prakesh, come on in. Mark's in the garden.

Prakesh: Thank you. Has Mark got his new goalpost?

Mother: Yes, he's been setting it up all morning.

Prakesh: He said he'd have it ready for this afternoon.

Narrator: Mark's mother took Prakesh through the house and into the back garden where Mark was tying up the net on his new goalpost.

Mother: Mark, Prakesh is here.

Mark: Hi Prakesh, what do you think about the goalpost?

Prakesh: It's neat! Get in goal and let me take some shots.

Mother: Don't let the ball go next door. Remember what Mr Blackmore is like about things going into his garden. He's just had a new greenhouse put up.

Mark: Don't worry, Mum, we'll keep the ball out of his precious garden.

Mother: Have a good game. I'll make a drink for you later.

Narrator: Mark's mother went indoors and the two boys began to kick a football around. Mark was the school goalkeeper so he went in goal first. Soon he was diving all over the grass saving Prakesh's shots.

Prakesh: It's Giggs running up to take the penalty, he shoots ... good save, Mark!

Mark: Come on, you can do better than that!

Prakesh: If I score will you let me go in goal?

Mark: All right, but you'll have to score first.

Narrator: Prakesh put the ball on the imaginary spot, took three steps back, carefully aimed and blasted the ball past Mark.

Prakesh: Yeah! What a goal!

Mark: What a lucky shot! I bet you couldn't do it again.

Prakesh: You said that I'd go in goal if I scored.

Mark: Okay, but if I score then we swap places again.

Narrator: Mark began to take shots at Prakesh but unfortunately Prakesh saved them all. Mark was getting really annoyed.

Prakesh: Come on Mark, I thought you could shoot!

Narrator: This really made Mark angry. He lined the ball up, ready to belt it really hard this time. He ran up to it and whacked it as hard as he could. But just as he kicked it his other foot slipped. The ball flew high over Prakesh's head. Mark watched in horror as the ball sailed over the fence into Mr Blackmore's garden. CRASH! There was a sound of glass breaking.

Mark: Oh no, I think it hit Mr Blackmore's greenhouse! Why didn't you stop it?

Prakesh: I'm not eight foot high, you know!

Narrator: The two boys ran over to the fence to see what they'd done. At the same time Mr Blackmore came out of his house. He looked very angry.

Mr Blackmore: What have you done this time?

Prakesh: I've just remembered, I have to go shopping for my Mum. I'll see you tomorrow, Mark.

Mark: Thanks a lot, Prakesh. I'm sorry Mr Blackmore, I didn't mean to break the glass in your greenhouse.

Mother: What has happened?

Mr Blackmore: I'm fed up with these footballs flying into my garden. Look at the damage this time.

Mother: Mark, I told you to be careful.

Mr Blackmore: He's broken at least three panes of glass in my greenhouse.

Mark: My foot slipped just as I was going to kick the ball. It wasn't supposed to go over the fence.

Mr Blackmore: Well, you're not getting your ball back until you have paid for new glass panes.

Mark: Prakesh should pay half.

Mother: Who kicked the ball?

Mark: I did.

Mother: Who was told to be careful?

Mark: I was.

Mother: Then you have to pay.

Mr Blackmore: I'll let you know later how much it will cost.

Narrator: That evening Mark's father was not very happy.

Father: Mr Blackmore says that the glass will cost £52.50. You'd better start saving up now, Mark.

Mark: I've only got two pounds.

Father: Well, you must save your three pounds a week pocket money. Then you'll have enough to pay Mr Blackmore in about 17 weeks.

Mark: That's not fair!

Father: Of course it is. What do you expect when you keep kicking your ball into his garden?

Narrator: Mark was very unhappy when he came home from school the next day. He usually went into the Post Office to buy a football magazine, but not that day. He was looking down as he passed the Post Office. Suddenly he noticed a small plastic bag on the pavement. He picked it up and saw that there was money inside it. He looked around to see if anybody had seen him. Then he slipped the plastic bag into his rucksack and ran home.

Mark: Twenty, forty, sixty pounds! I can pay Mr Blackmore his money and have some left over. Finders keepers, losers weepers!

Narrator: Mark hid the money away in his wardrobe. Later that evening Mark and his parents listened to the news. The newsreader said the government was thinking about increasing the old age pension. Sixty pounds was not enough for an old person to live on.

Father: It's about time they increased the pension. I don't know how pensioners manage on so little.

Mother: I agree. It's a shame they can't have more.

Narrator: Sixty pounds! That was exactly how much Mark had found. It must have belonged to an old-age pensioner. Mark knew he couldn't keep the money. The next day he stopped at the Post Office.

Shop Assistant: Can I help you young man?

Mark: Has anybody lost any money?

Shop Assistant: Why yes, I had a very worried lady in this morning. She told me she'd lost her housekeeping money.

Mark: How much was it?

Shop Assistant: I think she said that it was sixty pounds. Yes, she said that she lost three twenty-pound notes in a little plastic bag.

Mark: I've just found this bag on the road. It must be her money.

Shop Assistant: Well, thank you. What an honest person you are.

Mark: That's all right. I thought it might be somebody's pension.

Shop Assistant: You're right. You'll make the old lady very happy. What's your name so I can tell her?

Narrator: Mark told her his name and then went home. He still had no way of paying for the broken glass. When he got home he had quite a surprise. His father, mother and Mr Blackmore were waiting for him.

Father: Mark, we've just had a 'phone call from the Post Office. They told us that you'd handed in some lost money.

Mother: We're very proud of you.

Mr Blackmore: That money you found belonged to my wife. It was our week's housekeeping money.

Father: I think Mr Blackmore has a surprise for you.

Mr Blackmore: Yes, here is your football. Now don't worry about the broken glass. As a reward for your honesty you won't have to pay for the repairs.

Mother: Well done, Mark. But please be careful from now on when you play football in the garden!

Play 3

THE SMASHED PLANT

CHARACTERS

Narrator/Colin
Nina
Mrs Jones
Sereena
Pauline

SETTING

The children are sitting around two tables pushed together, drawing a large plant as part of an art lesson.

Sereena: This is better than doing Maths.

Nina: Anything's better than doing Maths! Actually, this is my favourite subject.

Colin: My favourite is football.

Nina: You're football mad.

Colin: So? What's wrong with that? When I'm a professional player I'll make more money than all of you put together.

Nina: Well, if I become a famous artist I'll sell my paintings for heaps of money. What about you, Pauline?

Pauline: I don't know. I think I'll get a job at Tesco. That's where my mum works.

Sereena: My uncle works there.

Mrs Jones: You've only got five more minutes so stop talking and get on with your work.

Colin: Pauline, I think you need some more red there.

Pauline: Leave it alone! Colin why did you do that? You're horrible.

Colin: Ha, ha, ha,ha ....

Sereena: Please miss, I've finished. What should I do with my painting?

Colin: I've finished as well. Can I go outside to play now?

Sereena: Your picture is a mess.

Mrs Jones: No it's not playtime yet, Colin. If you've finished your paintings, children, put them on the side. Here, I'll clear a space for you.

Narrator: Mrs Jones cleared a space for the finished paintings.

Mrs Jones: That's a good picture, Pauline, I like the green colour of the leaves.

Pauline: I'm not really very good. Nina helped me to mix the paint.

Mrs Jones: Thank you for helping, Nina. It looks as if everybody else except you is finished now.

Nina: Can I stay in at playtime and finish?

Pauline: Can I stay in as well?

Sereena: And me too?

Mrs Jones: You can stay in, Nina, just to finish off your painting. The rest of you can go out now. Don't make that face Pauline, you'll just chat to Nina and then she'll never finish her work.

Narrator: All the children except Nina went outside. She carried on finishing her painting of the large plant sitting in the centre of the two tables.

Nina: At least it is nice and peaceful now. OOPS! Oh no! I've dropped paint on the floor.

Narrator: Nina bent down to wipe the paint off the floor. She moved her table a little bit and suddenly something dropped by her head ... CRASH! The potted plant smashed onto the floor. It had been standing on the edges of the two tables. When Nina moved one table the plant fell down the gap.

Nina: Oh no, I don't believe it! Oh help, somebody's coming.

Narrator: Nina hid behind a bookcase. She didn't want to be caught with all that mess. Colin walked into the room.

Nina: (*to herself*): It's Colin, what does he want?

Colin: Now where did Mark say the football was? Oh yes, over in the corner, here it is. Hey what's all this mess? What's happened to the plant? Somebody's going to be in real trouble.

Nina: (*to herself*): I think I'd better get out of here.

Narrator: Nina waited for Colin to leave. Then she dashed outside and ran over to her friends.

Pauline: Are you all right?

Sereena: You look as if you've seen a ghost.

Nina: I've knocked over Mrs Jones' plant. It's smashed all over the floor!

Pauline: How did you do that?

Nina: I spilt some paint and when I tried to clean it up I moved one of the tables and it fell between them.

Sereena: What did Mrs Jones say?

Nina: She doesn't know yet.

Sereena: Mrs J will do her nut when she sees it!

Nina: What should I do?

Pauline: I'd keep quiet. Don't say anything.

Sereena: I think you should tell her. You'll get into trouble if you don't tell the truth.

Pauline: You'll be in bigger trouble if you do tell her. Did anybody see you?

Nina: Colin came in to get his football but I hid from him. So he didn't see me.

Pauline: Good, maybe we can blame him.

Sereena: That isn't very nice.

Pauline: He deserves it. He put red paint on my picture and spoiled it.

Narrator: The whistle blew for everyone to go back into their classrooms. Nina still didn't know what to do. When she walked into the classroom Mrs Jones was standing next to the broken plant with Colin.

Mrs Jones: Colin, you were seen in here with your football.

Colin: Honest, I didn't do anything.

Mrs Jones: You weren't playing football in the classroom were you?

Colin: No, the plant was already broken when I came in.

Pauline: Tell us another one, Colin.

Mrs Jones: Was anybody else in here when you came in?

Colin: No ... It's not fair, I get blamed for everything.

Pauline: Most of the time you are to blame.

Mrs Jones: That's enough, Pauline. Well, this is a real puzzle. I think we should have a talk about it again after school.

Colin: You never believe me.

Pauline: It serves you right. You're always horrible to us.

Sereena: Say something, Nina. It's not fair on Colin.

Nina: Yes, I know you're right. Mrs Jones, I've got something to tell you.

Play 4

THE DINNER LADY

CHARACTERS

Narrator
Nina/Mrs Jones
Colin
Mrs MacFee
Mark/Mr Hall

SETTING

The children in class J are not very happy because they are due to go on camp in three weeks' time and it looks as if it might be cancelled. This is because one of the parents who was hoping to supervise can no longer go.

Mrs Jones: Are you all sure you've all asked your parents if they can help?

Narrator: Mrs Jones had told the children to ask if any of their parents could go on the camp. But it looked as if the camp would have to be cancelled.

Mark: Why can't you and Mr Bell take us? Wouldn't two of you be enough?

Mrs Jones: I'm afraid the authority has a rule that there should be one adult for every ten children. I'm sure your Maths is good enough for you to work out that we'd need three adults for thirty children.

Colin: It isn't fair. I was really looking forward to going on camp.

Mark: Yeah, we've planned all year for this and now we can't go.

Colin: Why don't you take just twenty children?

Mark: Would you like to be one of the ones left behind?

Colin: I suppose not.

Mark: Why do we have to have adults with us anyway? It would be much more fun on our own!

Colin: That'd be great!

Mrs Jones: Oh yes, and how'd you get to the Centre without our help? Who'd do the cooking and patch up your poor little knee when you fell over and hurt yourself?

Narrator: The class laughed at that but when they went into the hall for lunch they were very quiet and sad as they sat down to eat.

Mrs MacFee: Oh dear, you lot don't look very happy.

Colin: We're not going on our camp.

Mrs MacFee: Why not?

Mark: We've only got two adults to go with us and we need three.

Mrs MacFee: Can't you get a parent to go with you?

Colin: No, we've tried that.

Nina: There's nobody else, it's not fair!

Mrs MacFee: How long was your camp?

Colin: It was only going to be three days.

Nina: It was going to be a long weekend, you know, leave Friday night and come back Sunday evening.

Mrs MacFee: Don't give up hope yet.

Narrator: After lunch Mrs Jones seemed rather excited and told the class to settle down quickly.

Mrs Jones: I've got some wonderful news for you.

Colin: Have we got the day off tomorrow?

Mrs Jones: Don't be silly, Colin. The camp is back on!

Mark: Who've you got to come along?

Mrs Jones: One of the dinner ladies, Mrs MacFee, has offered to come.

Colin: Hurrah for Mrs MacFee!

Narrator: The gloom in the classroom had suddenly been lifted and everybody was talking about going to camp.

Colin: I hope it'll be warm. We can have a water fight.

Mark: There's a super adventure play area near the camp site. I can't wait to go down the death slide.

Nina: I can't wait for the midnight feasts!

Narrator: A few days later it was very windy and wet outside. The children hadn't been able to get outside to play in the morning. They were all in a very silly mood. During the lunch break they began to be rude about Mrs MacFee who was a rather large lady who wore thick glasses.

Mark: What do you think it'll be like with Mrs MacFee on camp?

Colin: I hope she can cook.

Mark: She must eat well, look at the size of her.

Nina: Look out, here she comes.

Mrs MacFee: Hurry up and finish your lunch. We want to clean the tables.

Colin: Do you think there's a sleeping bag big enough for her?

Mark: I think we should sneak into her tent at night and steal her glasses.

Nina: Then when she gets up in the morning she won't see where she's going. She'll fall into the river.

Colin: Or down the outside loo!

Mrs MacFee: I don't know what you children are laughing at. Hurry up.

Mark: Maybe we can find a grass snake and put it into her sleeping bag.

Colin: Or a prickly hedgehog!

Mrs MacFee: I hope you're going to eat those grapes, Mark.

Colin: Her bed would be full of fleas.

Mark: She'd be scratching all day. Hey, he shoots, he scores!

Narrator: Mark carefully flicked a grape at Colin who flicked it back at him.

Colin: I bet you couldn't hit her on the back.

Mark: You just watch!

Mrs MacFee: What's going on? Are you throwing food?

Narrator: Mrs MacFee turned around to see what had hit her on the back. As she did so she put her foot down onto a grape that was on the floor. Her foot slipped out from under her and she fell down onto the floor with a heavy thump.

Mrs MacFee: Oh my ankle, help me somebody!

Nina: I'll go and get Mrs Jones.

Narrator: The children went very quiet as Mrs Jones came into the dining hall and helped Mrs MacFee up.

Mrs Jones: I'll see you lot later!

Colin: Now we're in trouble. Why did you throw the grape?

Mark: You told me to, so you're to blame as well.

Colin: It was your grape.

Narrator: The class worked very quietly that afternoon. At the end of the day Mr Hall came in.

Mrs Jones: Hello Mr Hall, how's Mrs MacFee?

Mr Hall: Not very well I'm afraid. Due to the stupidity of some of your class she has a broken ankle and will be off work for several weeks. This means she won't be able to go on camp. So I'm cancelling it.

Play 5

ONE TIN OF BAKED BEANS

CHARACTERS

Narrator
Mr Petrowski
Teacher/Sereena
Pauline
Colin/Dad

SETTING

It's the day before the Harvest service at school. The children are talking about the gifts of food they are going to bring for the main display.

Colin: I've got a bag full of tins of food. What have you got two got?

Sereena: I've got a bag of carrots, potatoes and a big marrow. What about you, Pauline?

Pauline: Oh, I haven't got mine yet, I'm getting it tonight. I'm hoping to bring a massive bag of apples.

Sereena: Have you got an apple tree in your garden?

Pauline: No, but I'll get some apples from the shop.

Narrator: Pauline felt herself go all hot inside because she was lying. She didn't know what she was going to give. When she got home that evening she spoke to her Dad.

Pauline: Dad, do we have any apples to spare for the school Harvest service tomorrow?

Dad: None at all, Pauline. Your Mum hasn't done the shopping yet.

Pauline: Do you think she'd get me some apples on the way home from work tonight?

Dad: We don't have money to spend on gifts for other people.

Pauline: But everyone will be bringing a gift of something. All the food is going to people who need it more than us.

Dad: There's a spare tin of baked beans in the cupboard. You can take that. It's all we've got.

Narrator: The next day Pauline put the tin of baked beans into her bag and set off for school. She was still worried because she'd told Sereena and Colin that she'd be bringing a bag of apples. As she passed Mr Petrowski's garden she looked over the fence.

Pauline: (*to herself*) Mr Petrowski has a big apple tree and it's full of apples. I wonder if I could get in there without him seeing me? He wouldn't miss one bagful.

Narrator: Pauline climbed over the fence and ran to the apple tree. She began to stuff apples into her bag. Then a hand grabbed her shoulder.

Mr Petrowski: What do you think you are doing, Missy?

Pauline: I'm, I'm borrowing some apples.

Mr Petrowski: You can't borrow an apple. Why are you coming into my garden like a thief? Come on, have you no tongue?

Pauline: I'm sorry, I only wanted to take a bag of apples for the school Harvest service. All I've got is a tin of baked beans. Everyone else is taking lots of things.

Mr Petrowski: Why didn't you ask first? You never know what you might get if you ask nicely.

Narrator: Mr Petrowski picked up her bag and tipped out the apples.

Mr Petrowski: Now let me see. This one's no good. You can't give this apple as a gift. It's been eaten by a bird. Here are eight good apples. Put them into your bag.

Pauline: Thank you very much, Mr Petrowski.

Mr Petrowski: Enjoy your Harvest. Now go out of my garden through the gate and not over the fence like a thief!

Narrator: Pauline was embarrassed by what had happened in Mr Petrowski's garden. But she was a lot happier. Now she was going to school with a bag full of apples as well as the tin of baked beans.

Teacher: Hello, Pauline. What have you got for our Harvest service?

Pauline: I've got a tin of baked beans and a bag of apples.

Teacher: They look lovely apples. I am sure somebody will enjoy the baked beans too. Did the apples come from your garden?

Narrator: Pauline felt very embarrassed by that question. She thought about what Mr Petrowski had said about going into his garden like a thief.

Pauline: No, a neighbour gave them to me.

Teacher: Well, that was very kind of him. I hope you thanked him?

Pauline: Yes, I did.

Colin: I see you got your apples.

Teacher: Everyone settle down for register now.

Colin: Please, Miss, are we going to deliver the boxes of food to the elderly?

Teacher: Yes, Colin. We'll be doing that later.

Narrator: At the end of the day all the food from the Harvest service was put into boxes for the children to deliver. Pauline, Sereena and Colin had two boxes to deliver. Pauline couldn't believe the name on the first box.

Pauline: I know Mr Petrowski, he lives around the corner from me.

Colin: That's a funny name. Where does he come from?

Sereena: Doesn't he live on his own? I think he comes from Poland.

Pauline: Yes, that's right.

Narrator: The children set off with the two boxes. First they delivered a box to an elderly couple. They were very pleased with the gift of food. Then they went on to Mr Petrowski's home.

Pauline: Colin, you knock on the door.

Colin: Why, are you afraid of him?

Pauline: No, it's not that ...

Sereena: I'll knock on the door.

Mr Petrowski: Why hello, what do we have here?

Colin: We had our Harvest service today.

Sereena: We collected some food for you.

Mr Petrowski: Well, that's very kind of you. Look at these lovely apples.

Sereena: Pauline gave those, didn't you, Pauline?

Pauline: Yes.

Mr Petrowski: That's very kind of you. Oh look! I can see my favourite food in the box. I love baked beans. Thank you very much. I'll really enjoy those for my tea.

Colin: Goodbye.

Sereena: Goodbye.

Pauline: Goodbye Mr Petrowski and ... thank you.